T0363834

KANPAI!
かんぱい!

KANPAI!

かんぱい!

NAOMI COLEMAN

Illustrations by Phil Constantinesco

Smith Street Books

PART ONE
パート 1 サニーデーズ

PART TWO
パート 2 心地よい夜

PART THREE
パート 3 夜更かし

はじめに Introduction

From street corners where voices float out of izakaya to hotel bars that peer over cities and vending machines that sell beer and chu-hai, Japan's drinking culture has captured international imagination. Its master bartenders have garnered a reputation for precision, known for carefully carved ice and the consideration that goes into every step of building a drink. This starts with equipment and ends with cocktails prepared with practised movements and a respect for ritual, simple recipes the subject of a years-long pursuit of mastery.

Japan's pursuit of perfection in cocktails doesn't start with the bartenders, however: it begins with the alcohols that the country makes. These are prepared with produce carefully tended to – an attention that's present in the botanical notes of the country's gins, the smoothness of its whiskies and the unique flavours of its liqueurs.

Kanpai! is a celebration of these flavours, and of a mixology history that stretches back to 1874. That year, the International Hotel in Yokohama opened Japan's

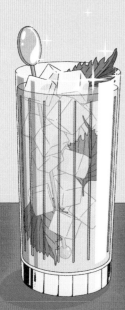

first cocktail bar. Soon after in 1890, German bartender Louis Eppinger arrived to help usher cocktails into the country, heading up the bar at Yokohama's Grand Hotel. He popularised both the Million Dollar (page 50) and the Bamboo (page 66) during his time there.

More than a century later, the venues serving cocktails in Japan have exploded to comprise myriad bars, from hushed rooms where drinks are sipped slowly, to louder spaces where service takes place beside dancefloors. The menus that serve these venues vary, some featuring classics such as Martinis, others more casual drinks like the Cassis Orange (page 106). *Kanpai!* captures some of these favourites, alongside cocktails invented in Japan, including the Kaikan Fizz (page 20).

Many of this book's recipes are new, however, taking inspiration from Japan's alcohols, gardens and pantries to create riffs like a Sake 75 (page 44) and a Sakura Martini (page 102). Others nod to staples of Japanese culture, with boozy parfaits (pages 30 and 46) and a Melon Soda (page 96). Some recipes are perfect for lazy brunches, like the Spumoni (page 42), some for curling up next to a fire, including the Hojicha Toddy (page 84), and others for the late hours on long nights, like the Gulf Stream (page 90). With each of its 50 cocktails, *Kanpai!* celebrates a slice of Japan, from the flavours that define its sweets and dishes to the drinks that its bartenders invented and the classics that their patrons love.

A note on Japanese alcohol

Japan is home to many alcohols. Some hail from the country, including sake and shochu, while some are infused with Japanese methods and flavours, including their locally produced gin. Throughout *Kanpai!*, many alcohols can be substituted with those bottled in other countries, but for the fullest experience, Japanese brands are recommended.

Note: all recipes in *Kanpai!* serve one.

ANZUSHU

Anzushu is a liqueur made with meticulously grown Japanese apricots. Like the other liqueurs listed here, it has a low alcohol content, making it an excellent addition to cocktails enjoyed during the daytime.

GIN

There is a wealth of native botanicals in Japan suited to gin. Local distillers enhance the alcohol's base juniper flavour with ingredients like cherry blossom, sansho pepper and yuzu. Each gin imparts unique flavours to cocktails, so experiment with different types to find your favourites.

MIDORI

Midori is a sweet melon liqueur. It is not usually consumed on its own but is used as a cocktail base. Its bright green colour adds an unmistakable hue to the drinks it's mixed into.

MOMOSHU

Momoshu is a liqueur made with Japanese white peaches, which lend it a delightfully smooth, sweet taste that's perfect mixed into alcohols, or simply sipped on its own.

SAKE

Japan's national beverage is created using only four ingredients: rice, koji, yeast and water. There's a world of sake to explore, with many different varieties. Some are best served hot, some cold and many offer a delicious base for cocktails.

SHOCHU

Compared to other traditional Japanese offerings, shochu has a higher alcohol content. It is a clear, distilled liquor, which is made by first fermenting the base ingredient, which can be rice, sweet potato or barley, among many other options. Depending on this ingredient, and how long the shochu is aged, the resulting alcohol varies widely, some shochu subtle, some floral, some sweet, and some more robust in flavour.

UMESHU

Made from the ume plum, umeshu is often referred to as a wine but is best described as a liqueur. The green plums are steeped in sugar and alcohol, producing this sweet, versatile treat.

WHISKY

Japanese whisky has a unique flavour all of its own. Building on over 100 years of local tradition, contemporary distillers produce whisky with less peat than their Scottish counterparts, though they use the same methods. The result is a spirit known for its light, smooth finish.

YUZUSHU

Yuzu, including the peels, are steeped in sake and sweetened with sugar to produce yuzushu. The liqueur adds a wonderful dimension to citrus-forward cocktails like Margaritas.

A note on Japanese ingredients

Throughout *Kanpai!*, ingredients like matcha and yuzu are used to transform drinks. While some are easily found in most supermarkets, others, like shiso, will likely need to be purchased from an Asian grocer.

CALPICO
Easily found in Japan's famous vending machines, Calpico (also sold as Calpis) is a popular milk based non carbonated drink. There are many varieties available, but most have a sweet and tangy flavour.

MATCHA
Matcha is a powder made from ground tea leaves. With an earthy flavour, it is traditionally brewed to drink but is also delicious added to desserts.

MISO
Miso is a fermented soybean paste which is famous for its umami flavour. It is extremely versatile and is a key ingredient in Japanese cuisine.

SAKURA
The much-loved cherry blossom is symbolic of Japan, celebrated in spring with festivals all over the country. The beautiful flowers are also used as botanicals in Japanese gin.

SHISO
Shiso is a type of mint and a popular herb in Japan. Its leaves have a flavour that sits in the realm of mint, cloves, liquorice and cinnamon.

WASABI
This paste is made from the root of the wasabi plant, which is native to Japan. It is known around the world as an accompaniment to sashimi, but it also works well in cocktails that require a kick of heat.

YUZU
Yuzu is a citrus fruit native to parts of East Asia that balances sweetness with sharpness. It tastes like a blend of lemon, orange and grapefruit. If you are unable to source a yuzu, lemon juice can be used in this book's recipes.

パート1 サニーデーズ

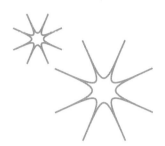

PART ONE

Sunny Days

When the blue sky invites you to spread out a picnic blanket in a park or to gather on the patio for brunch, these drinks are the perfect complement to a lazy day spent in the sun.

MOMO SPRITZ

Japan's famous attention to detail is present in the way its peaches are grown: covered in small paper bags to encourage sweetness and to maintain a pale colour. These carefully tended fruits produce momoshu, a liqueur which is quite the treat alone, or paired with Prosecco and gin. If sakura gin is hard to find, regular gin can be used.

ICE CUBES
25 ML (¾ OZ) MOMOSHU
2 TABLESPOONS SAKURA GIN
100 ML (3½ OZ) PROSECCO
SPARKLING WATER, TO TOP
PEACH SLICE, TO GARNISH

Fill a wine glass with ice, then pour in the momoshu, gin and Prosecco. Gently stir to combine.

Finish with a splash of sparkling water and garnish with the peach slice.

COCKTAIL NO. 01

桃スプリッツ

Momo
Spritz

TOKYO COLLINS

Unlike a Tom Collins, which uses lemon juice, this Tokyo Collins heroes yuzu. The drink's simplicity makes it the perfect chance to showcase the native botanicals of your favourite dry Japanese gin.

ICE CUBES
60 ML (2 OZ) GIN
2 TABLESPOONS YUZU JUICE
1 TABLESPOON SIMPLE SYRUP (PAGE 118)
SPARKLING WATER, TO TOP
3 RASPBERRIES, TO GARNISH

Fill a cocktail shaker with ice, then pour in the gin, yuzu juice and simple syrup and shake until chilled.

Strain into an ice-filled Collins glass and top up with sparkling water.

Garnish with the raspberries.

COCKTAIL NO. 02

東京コリンズ

Tokyo Collins

SHOCHU MARY

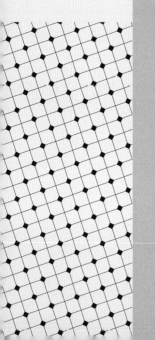

There's a lot to savour in this Bloody Mary. To start, the glass is rimmed with shichimi togarashi, a moreish spice mix with a kick. Then there's the complexity shochu adds, the alcohol pairing beautifully with the other layers of flavours. And finally there's a hit of wasabi to sharpen the senses, making this drink the perfect chaser to a late night out.

SHICHIMI TOGARASHI, TO RIM THE GLASS
1 LEMON WEDGE, PLUS 20 ML (¾ OZ) LEMON JUICE
ICE CUBES
50 ML (1¾ OZ) SHOCHU
½ TEASPOON WASABI POWDER
125 ML (½ CUP) TOMATO JUICE
2 DASHES OF TABASCO
2 DASHES OF WORCESTERSHIRE SAUCE
1 DASH OF SOY SAUCE
OLIVE, TO GARNISH

Tip shichimi togarashi into a shallow dish. Moisten the rim of a highball glass with the lemon wedge, then dip or roll the edge of the glass in the shichimi togarashi to coat.

Fill the prepared glass with ice, then add the remaining ingredients except the olive. Stir to combine, and season with salt and pepper.

Garnish with the olive.

COCKTAIL NO. 03

焼酎マリー

Shochu
Mary

KAIKAN FIZZ

The story goes that after World War II, General Douglas MacArthur entered a Tokyo bar one morning and was shocked to see soldiers on the sauce before lunch. Not wanting to lose their thirsty customers, the bartenders concocted a cocktail that looks exactly like a glass of milk – problem solved!

ICE CUBES
70 ML (2¼ OZ) NAVY STRENGTH GIN
1 TABLESPOON LEMON JUICE
1½ TEASPOONS SIMPLE SYRUP (PAGE 118)
2 TABLESPOONS MILK
SPARKLING WATER, TO TOP

Fill a cocktail shaker with ice, then pour in the remaining ingredients, except the sparkling water, and shake vigorously until chilled.

Strain into a highball glass filled with ice and top up with sparkling water.

COCKTAIL NO. 04

會館フィズ

Kaikan Fizz

M I L K   T E A

Since the mid-1960s, Milk Tea has been a staple of Japanese culture. Prepared on the stove in a saucepan, or made with instant powder, it is marked by a high ratio of milk to water and isn't shy of sugar. To create a cocktail spin on the classic, just add whisky and vanilla syrup for a warming sipper. For those looking to make the recipe quicker, you can find milk tea powder at an Asian grocer.

1½ TEASPOONS BLACK TEA LEAVES (ASSAM, CEYLON OR DARJEELING)
125 ML (½ CUP) MILK
2 TABLESPOONS JAPANESE WHISKY
VANILLA SYRUP (PAGE 118), TO TASTE

In a small saucepan, bring 125 ml (½ cup) of water to a simmer. Reduce the heat to low and add the tea leaves. Cover and steep for 2–3 minutes, depending on your desired strength.

Add the milk and bring back up to a simmer. Remove from the heat and strain into a teacup.

Add the whisky and vanilla syrup and stir to combine.

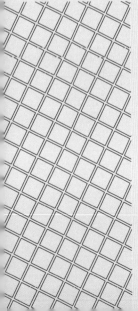

COCKTAIL NO. 05

ミルクティー

Milk
Tea

SHISO MOJITO

The Mojito is a summery favourite that's hard to go past. For a Japanese spin on the classic, simply switch two of the key ingredients: substitute the mint with shiso and the rum with shochu. This twist produces a light drink with an aromatic and bright taste.

25 ML (¾ OZ) LIME JUICE
1 TABLESPOON GINGER SYRUP (PAGE 118)
3 GREEN SHISO LEAVES, PLUS 1 LEAF TO GARNISH
ICE CUBES
3 TABLESPOONS SHOCHU
SPARKLING WATER, TO TOP

Gently muddle the lime juice, ginger syrup and shiso leaves in a highball glass.

Fill the glass with ice, then pour in the shochu and stir to combine.

Top up with sparkling water and garnish with the remaining shiso leaf.

COCKTAIL NO. 06

紫蘇モヒート

Shiso
Mojito

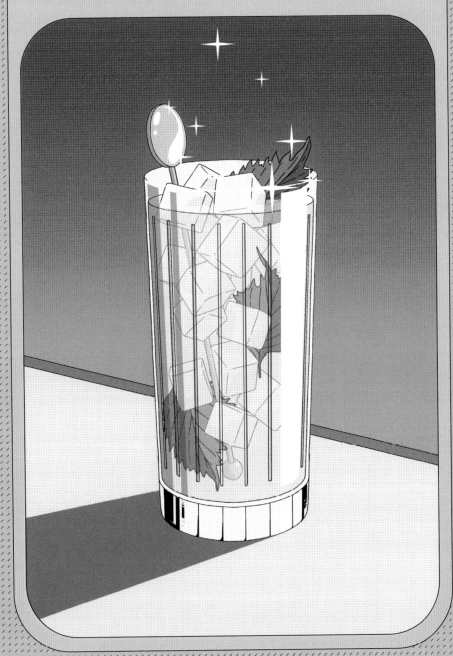

ICHIGO SPRITZ

Ichigo (strawberries) are popular in Japan for good reason: they are exceptionally delicious due to careful cultivation in greenhouses, picked at peak ripeness. In this recipe, the fruit is allowed to shine with the help of sake and Champagne in a fragrant spritz.

3–4 STRAWBERRIES, PLUS 1–2 SLICED
   STRAWBERRIES TO GARNISH
2 TABLESPOONS YUZU JUICE
ICE CUBES
3 TABLESPOONS SAKE
100 ML (3½ OZ) CHAMPAGNE

Muddle the strawberries with the yuzu juice in a cocktail shaker. Pour into an ice-filled wine glass, then add the sake and stir to combine.

Finish with the Champagne and garnish with the sliced strawberries.

苺スプリッツ

**Ichigo
Spritz**

MOMOSHU BELLINI

Created to sip at brunch, a Bellini is a bubbly way to start the morning. The classic peach puree is complemented in this version by momoshu for a simple twist on the staple.

1 PEACH, PLUS 1 SLICE TO GARNISH
3 TABLESPOONS MOMOSHU
PROSECCO, TO TOP

Blitz the peach in a blender until smooth, adding a little Prosecco to loosen up the peach if necessary.

Spoon 60 g (2 oz) of the peach puree into a champagne flute. Pour in the momoshu and top up with Prosecco. Stir gently to combine.

Garnish with the peach slice.

Any left-over puree can be kept in an airtight container in the fridge for up to five days.

COCKTAIL NO. 08

桃酒ベリーニ

Momoshu
Bellini

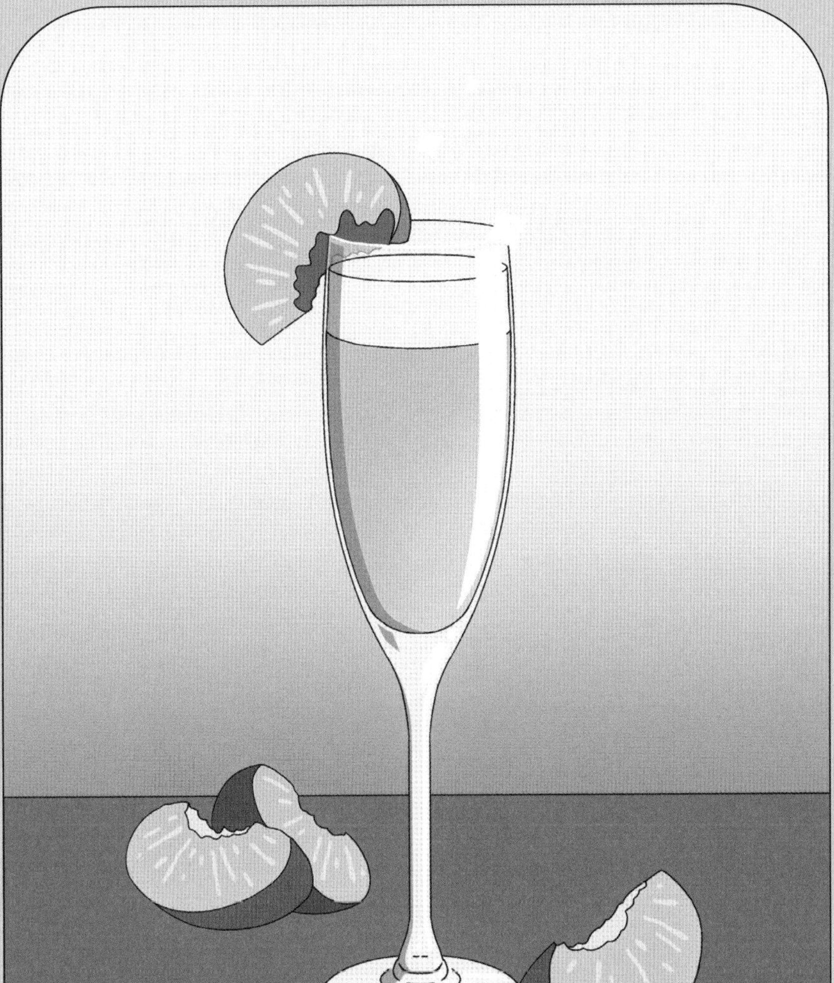

FRUIT PARFAIT

In Japan, parfaits are served piled high, these bright and colourful confections built from layers of ice cream, whipped cream and other treats like sliced fruit, perched glistening on top. However, unlike in the parfaits enjoyed in Japan's dessert parlours, this one features alcoholic jellies at the bottom of the glass.

8–12 FRUIT JELLY SQUARES (PAGE 119)
2 SCOOPS OF VANILLA ICE CREAM
1 TABLESPOON FRUIT JAM OF YOUR CHOICE
   (OPTIONAL)
60 ML (¼ CUP) WHIPPED CREAM (PAGE 119)
SLICED FRUIT OF YOUR CHOICE

Place the jelly squares in a parfait glass, then top with a scoop of the ice cream.

Layer with the jam, if using, then top with the remaining scoop of ice cream and the whipped cream.

Finish with the sliced fruits.

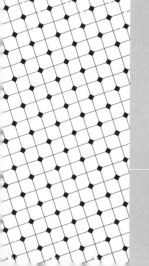

フルーツパフェ

Fruit
Parfait

ANZU DAIQUIRI

Traditionally, a Daiquiri is made of three ingredients: rum, lime and sugar – a tart, sweet base that's a great complement for anzushu. This apricot liqueur adds a burst of sunshine to the glass, elevating the complexity of this cocktail classic.

ICE CUBES
50 ML (1¾ OZ) WHITE RUM
2 TEASPOONS ANZUSHU
1 TABLESPOON LIME JUICE
½ TEASPOON SIMPLE SYRUP (PAGE 118)
APRICOT SLICE, TO GARNISH

Fill a cocktail shaker with ice, then pour in the liquids and shake until chilled.

Strain into a chilled coupe glass and garnish with the apricot slice.

COCKTAIL NO. 10

杏ダイキリ

Anzu
Daiquiri

STRAWBERRY MILK

Across Japan, you'll commonly find strawberry milk – a crowd favourite. In a nod to the classic sweet drink, this cocktail features strawberry-flavoured Calpico. Its tangy, creamy flavour lends itself to a delicious drink that's perfect enjoyed in the summer, when strawberries are at their juiciest.

3 STRAWBERRIES, PLUS 1 STRAWBERRY
   TO GARNISH
ICE CUBES
40 ML (1¼ OZ) VODKA
100 ML (3½ OZ) CALPICO, STRAWBERRY FLAVOUR

Blitz the strawberries in a blender until smooth, loosening with Calpico if necessary.

Fill a tumbler with ice, then spoon in the strawberry puree. Pour in the vodka and Calpico and stir to combine.

Garnish with the remaining strawberry.

COCKTAIL NO. 11

苺牛乳

Strawberry
Milk

CASSIS SPRITZ

Creme de cassis is a popular liqueur in Japan with a fruity, sweet flavour that's made with blackcurrants. What better way to enjoy this juicy, jewel-toned treat than by mixing it with Prosecco for an effervescent spritz?

ICE CUBES
2 TABLESPOONS CREME DE CASSIS
115 ML (4 OZ) PROSECCO
SPARKLING WATER, TO TOP
3 BLACKCURRANTS AND AN ORANGE TWIST,
    TO GARNISH

Fill a wine glass with ice. Pour in the creme de cassis and Prosecco and stir gently to combine.

Top up with sparkling water and garnish with the blackcurrants and orange twist.

COCKTAIL NO. 12

カシス スプリッツ

Cassis Spritz

EYE CANDY

The Eye Candy lends itself to a Japanese twist with the substitution of its two fresh ingredients: ginger and mint. Just switch out the ginger for Japanese native myoga, which is more delicate in taste, and the mint for shiso, which introduces notes that include cinnamon.

3 SLICES OF MYOGA
4 SHISO LEAVES, PLUS 1–2 LEAVES TO GARNISH
1 TABLESPOON SIMPLE SYRUP (PAGE 118)
3 TABLESPOONS GIN
1 TABLESPOON ELDERFLOWER LIQUEUR
1 TABLESPOON LEMON JUICE
ICE CUBES
SPARKLING WATER, TO TOP

Gently muddle the myoga, shiso leaves and simple syrup in a cocktail shaker.

Pour in the gin, elderflower liqueur and lemon juice and fill the shaker with ice. Shake until chilled and strain into an ice-filled tumbler.

Top up with sparkling water and garnish with the remaining shiso leaves.

COCKTAIL NO. 13

アイ キャンディ

Eye Candy

MISO DAIQUIRI

This cocktail plays on the traditional Daiquiri by introducing sudachi juice and miso. Sudachi is a sour citrus often used in Japanese cooking, but combined here with a miso syrup, it gives this cocktail a peppery tang. If you can't find the fruit, lime juice can be used instead.

ICE CUBES
50 ML (1¾ OZ) WHITE RUM
2 TABLESPOONS SUDACHI
20 ML (¾ OZ) MISO SYRUP (PAGE 118)
LIME TWIST, TO GARNISH

Fill a cocktail shaker with ice, then add all the ingredients except the lime twist. Shake until chilled.

Strain into a chilled coupe glass and garnish with the lime twist.

COCKTAIL NO. 14

味噌ダイキリ

Miso
Daiquiri

SPUMONI

Not to be confused with the layered gelato treat from the United States, the Spumoni cocktail originated in Japan. It's a low-alcohol sipper featuring the deliciously tart Italian aperitif Campari – perfect for a long, lazy day of drinking.

ICE CUBES
3 TABLESPOONS CAMPARI
3 TABLESPOONS PINK GRAPEFRUIT JUICE
TONIC WATER, TO TOP
PINK GRAPEFRUIT SLICE, TO GARNISH

Fill a highball glass with ice, then pour in the Campari and grapefruit juice.

Top up with tonic water and stir to combine. Garnish with the grapefruit slice.

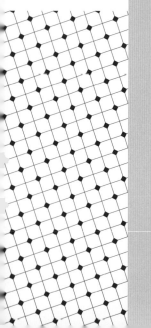

スプモーニ　Spumoni

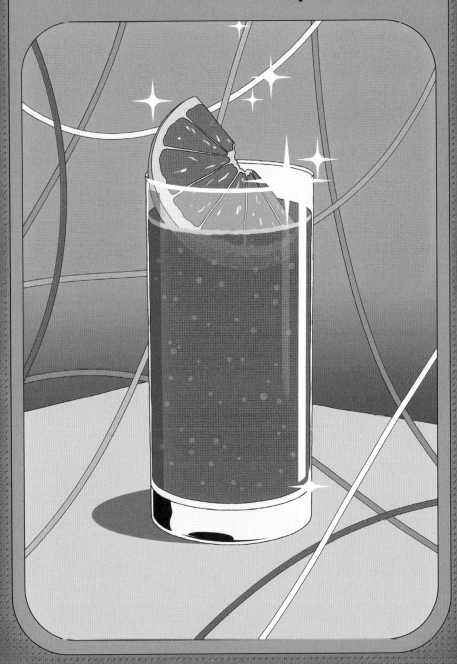

SAKE 75

Hailing from Paris, the French 75 is a 20th-century classic that features Champagne. In this version, however, sparkling sake is paired with the gin for a bubbly riff on the original.

ICE CUBES
2 TABLESPOONS GIN
1 TABLESPOON LEMON JUICE
1 TABLESPOON SIMPLE SYRUP (PAGE 118)
SPARKLING SAKE, TO TOP
LEMON TWIST, TO GARNISH

Fill a cocktail shaker with ice, then pour in the gin, lemon juice and simple syrup and shake until chilled.

Strain the drink into a champagne flute and top up with sake.

Garnish with the lemon twist.

酒75

Sake 75

MATCHA PARFAIT

Like the Fruit Parfait on page 30, this Matcha Parfait plays on Japan's extravagant, layered desserts with the inclusion of alcoholic jellies. Layered on top is ice cream, matcha cream and ogura-an (sweetened red beans), which you can find in tinsat Asian grocers. Anko, which is a paste made from red beans, can also be used.

8–12 MATCHA JELLY SQUARES (PAGE 119)
2 SCOOPS VANILLA OR MATCHA ICE CREAM
1 TABLESPOON OGURA-AN
60 ML (¼ CUP) MATCHA CREAM (PAGE 119)

Place half of the matcha jellies into a parfait glass, then top with the ice cream.

Add the rest of the jellies, then finish with the ogura-an and matcha cream.

抹茶パフェ

Matcha Parfait

パート2 心地よい夜

PART TWO

Cosy Eve- nings

On colder evenings, curl up under a blanket with any of these drinks, perfect for enjoying with loved ones as you listen to rain pattering away on the roof.

MILLION DOLLAR

The Million Dollar was one of the original cocktails created in Japan by Louis Eppinger, a German bartender working in Yokohama starting in the 1890s. With its smooth and fruity balance, it's no wonder Eppinger's creation helped cocktails take hold in the country.

60 ML (¼ CUP) GIN
2 TABLESPOONS SWEET VERMOUTH
1 TABLESPOON PINEAPPLE JUICE
1 TEASPOON GRENADINE
1 EGG WHITE OR 2 TABLESPOONS AQUAFABA
ICE CUBES
PINEAPPLE WEDGE, TO GARNISH

Add all the liquids to a cocktail shaker and shake vigorously to emulsify the egg. Add ice and shake again until chilled.

Strain into a chilled coupe glass and garnish with the pineapple wedge.

COCKTAIL NO. 18

ミリオン・ダラー

Million
Dollar

Y U Z U B E E

The Bee's Knees originated in Paris and made its cocktail book debut in 1929. Its mix of gin, lemon and honey, which has stood the test of time, is simple enough to easily riff on. Here, yuzu recreates the drink with a unique tang, introduced through gin and juice, for a subtle twist on a classic.

ICE CUBES
3 TABLESPOONS YUZU GIN
1 TABLESPOON HONEY
25 ML (¾ OZ) YUZU JUICE
YUZU TWIST, TO GARNISH

Fill a cocktail shaker with ice, then pour in all the ingredients, except the yuzu twist, and shake until chilled.

Strain into a chilled coupe glass and garnish with the yuzu twist.

COCKTAIL NO. 19

柚子ビー

Yuzu
Bee

KURI OLD FASHIONED

In Japan, you'll find chestnuts added to dishes, including many desserts. Here, the nut elevates the Old Fashioned via liqueur, which gives the drink a subtle, nutty flavour, perfect for imbibing on crisp autumn days.

ICE CUBES, PLUS LARGE ICE CUBE TO SERVE
50 ML (1¾ OZ) JAPANESE WHISKY
1 TABLESPOON CHESTNUT LIQUEUR
2 DASHES OF ANGOSTURA BITTERS
ORANGE TWIST, TO GARNISH

Fill a mixing glass with ice, then pour in the liquids and stir until chilled.

Place the large ice cube in an old fashioned glass, then strain in the drink from the mixing glass.

Garnish with the orange twist.

COCKTAIL NO. 20

昔風の栗

Kuri Old
Fashioned

LITTLE TOKYO

This Manhattan receives a twist with the introduction of sake, which makes for a drink that's not as heavy as the 19th-century original. The rice wine paired with vermouth and whisky creates layers best enjoyed slowly.

ICE CUBES
60 ML (¼ CUP) SAKE
2 TABLESPOONS JAPANESE WHISKY
1 TABLESPOON SWEET VERMOUTH
2 DASHES OF ANGOSTURA BITTERS
BRANDIED CHERRY, TO GARNISH

Fill a mixing glass with ice, then pour in the liquids and stir until chilled.

Strain into a chilled coupe glass and garnish with the cherry.

COCKTAIL NO. 21

リトル東京

Little
Tokyo

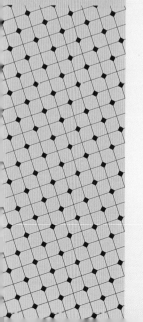

KAKI SOUR

Japan's beloved kaki (persimmon) indicates the coming of autumn and cooler evenings. With its honey-like flavour, the fruit is the perfect partner for gin in a sour.

1 PERSIMMON, PEELED AND SEEDED, PLUS A SLICE
   TO GARNISH
2 TABLESPOONS SIMPLE SYRUP (PAGE 118)
ICE CUBES
2 TABLESPOONS LEMON JUICE
50 ML (1¾ OZ) GIN
1 STAR ANISE, TO GARNISH (OPTIONAL)

Blitz the persimmon and simple syrup in a blender until smooth.

Fill a cocktail shaker with ice, then add 3 tablespoons of the persimmon puree, the lemon juice and gin, and shake until chilled.

Strain into an ice-filled old fashioned glass. Garnish with the star anise, if desired, and the persimmon slice.

Any left-over puree can be kept in an airtight container in the fridge for up to five days.

COCKTAIL NO. 22

柿サワー

Kaki
Sour

MOUNT FUJI

The Mount Fuji originated at the Imperial Hotel in Tokyo in 1924 where it was served to cruise ship passengers who stopped over at the Frank Lloyd Wright–designed building. In a nod to the famous mountain, the cocktail's colour symbolises snow, and the cherry, the rising sun.

50 ML (1¾ OZ) GIN
1 TEASPOON MARASCHINO LIQUEUR
1 TABLESPOON LEMON JUICE
1 TEASPOON PINEAPPLE JUICE
1 TEASPOON SIMPLE SYRUP (PAGE 118)
1 EGG WHITE OR 2 TABLESPOONS AQUAFABA
2 TEASPOONS CREAM
ICE CUBES
MARASCHINO CHERRY, TO GARNISH

Pour all the ingredients, except the ice and cherry, into a cocktail shaker and shake vigorously to emulsify the egg. Add ice and shake again until chilled.

Strain into a chilled coupe glass and garnish with the cherry.

Kanpai!

COCKTAIL NO. 23

富士山

Mount
Fuji

UME NEGRONI

A Negroni is one of the easiest cocktails to make, given there are only three ingredients, all served in equal measures, and with no cocktail shaker required. To introduce a new flavour to the Italian classic, this version replaces the vermouth with umeshu, this plum liqueur pairing beautifully with the bitter citrus of Campari.

LARGE ICE CUBE
2 TABLESPOONS JAPANESE GIN
2 TABLESPOONS UMESHU
2 TABLESPOONS CAMPARI
ORANGE TWIST, TO GARNISH

Place the ice cube in a tumbler, then pour in the liquids and stir to combine.

Garnish with the orange twist.

梅ネグローニ

Ume
Negroni

SOUTHERN SUMMER

This peach-flavoured sipper features kuromitsu, which is a syrup made with Okinawan black sugar. Commonly found in desserts, its rich flavour is also delicious paired with bourbon. Kuromitsu can be purchased at Asian grocers.

ICE CUBES
60 ML (¼ CUP) BOURBON
20 ML (¾ OZ) KUROMITSU
2 TABLESPOONS MOMOSHU
PEACH SLICE AND MINT LEAF, TO GARNISH

Fill a cocktial shaker with ice, then pour in the liquids and shake until chilled.

Strain into an ice-filled rocks glass and garnish with the peach slice and mint leaf.

南部の夏

Southern
Summer

BAMBOO

During his time working in Yokohama, Louis Eppinger, known for the Million Dollar (page 50), also popularised the Bamboo. While the drink is always made with sherry and vermouth, recipes combine them in varying ratios. Here, the two are matched one for one, but try reducing the vermouth if you'd like to experiment.

ICE CUBES
3 TABLESPOONS FINO SHERRY
3 TABLESPOONS DRY VERMOUTH
2 DASHES OF ANGOSTURA BITTERS
2 DASHES OF ORANGE BITTERS
ORANGE TWIST, TO GARNISH

Fill a mixing glass with ice, then pour in the liquids and stir until chilled.

Strain into a chilled coupe glass and garnish with the orange twist.

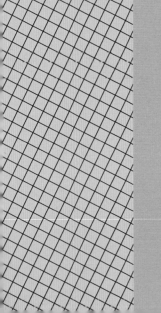

竹   **Bamboo**

SAKURA CLUB

This cocktail riffs on the beloved Clover Club, famous for its tart raspberry flavour. Here, the fruit is paired with the floral notes of sakura gin in a pink-hued nod to the springtime blossoms.

4 RASPBERRIES
1 TABLESPOON SIMPLE SYRUP (PAGE 118)
60 ML (¼ CUP) SAKURA GIN
1 TABLESPOON LEMON JUICE
1 EGG WHITE OR 2 TABLESPOONS AQUAFABA
ICE CUBES
CHERRY BLOSSOM, TO GARNISH

Muddle the raspberries with the simple syrup in a cocktail shaker. Add the remaining ingredients, except the ice and cherry blossom, and shake vigorously to emulsify the egg. Add ice and shake again until chilled.

Strain into a chilled cocktail glass and garnish with the cherry blossom.

桜倶楽部

Sakura Club

Y U Z U   S O U R

What better way to spotlight two delicious Japanese cocktail ingredients than with a whisky sour? This Yuzu Sour blends the smooth taste of Japanese whisky with the sharp tang of the yuzu for a fragrant, balanced cocktail.

60 ML (¼ CUP) JAPANESE WHISKY
2 TABLESPOONS YUZU JUICE
1 TABLESPOON SIMPLE SYRUP (PAGE 118)
1 EGG WHITE OR 2 TABLESPOONS AQUAFABA
ICE CUBES, PLUS 1–2 LARGE ICE CUBES TO SERVE
2–3 DASHES OF ANGOSTURA BITTERS,
   TO GARNISH

Pour the liquids, except the bitters, into a cocktail shaker and shake vigorously to emulsify the egg. Add ice and shake again until chilled.

Place the large ice cubes in a rocks glass, then strain in the drink from the shaker.

Garnish with the bitters.

柚子サワー

Yuzu Sour

KISS OF FIRE

Kenji Ishioka won a Japanese bartending competition in 1953 with the Kiss of Fire. Aptly named, it has a high-alcohol content which will light up your throat. To offset the alcoholic punch and give a sweetness to each sip, the glass is rimmed with sugar.

SUGAR, TO RIM THE GLASS
WEDGE OF LEMON
ICE CUBES
20 ML (¾ OZ) VODKA
20 ML (¾ OZ) SLOE GIN
20 ML (¾ OZ) DRY VERMOUTH

Tip the sugar into a shallow dish. Moisten the rim of a chilled coupe glass with the lemon wedge, then dip or roll the edge of the glass in the sugar to coat.

Fill a cocktail shaker with ice, then pour in the remaining ingredients and shake until chilled.

Strain the drink into the prepared coupe.

COCKTAIL NO. 29

キス オブ ファイヤー

Kiss of
Fire

NASHI MARTINI

Distinct in shape and taste from other pears, a ripe Nashi pear is crisp and juicy: the perfect addition to a cocktail when you're looking for something refreshing. Here, the fruit is partnered with ginger for a drink that's pleasantly warming and sweet.

1 NASHI PEAR, ROUGHLY CHOPPED, PLUS 1 SLICE
   TO GARNISH
ICE CUBES
3 TABLESPOONS JAPANESE GIN
1 TEASPOON GINGER SYRUP (PAGE 118)

Muddle the pear in a cocktail shaker to extract the juice. Fine strain the juice into a glass and discard the solids.

Fill the cocktail shaker with ice, then pour in 3 tablespoons of the pear juice along with the gin and ginger syrup and shake until chilled.

Strain into a chilled cocktail glass and garnish with the pear slice.

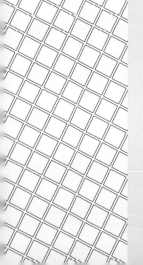

COCKTAIL NO. 30

梨マティーニ

Nashi
Martini

TAKUMI'S AVIATION

Takumi Watanabe represented Japan in the 2010 Diageo World Class Bartender competition. He impressed the judges with his version of the Aviation, which is now a contemporary classic, and an arguably better drink than the original.

ICE CUBES
3 TABLESPOONS GIN
1 TABLESPOON MARASCHINO LIQUEUR
1 TEASPOON PARFAIT AMOUR
2 TEASPOONS LEMON JUICE
LEMON TWIST, TO GARNISH

Fill a cocktail shaker with ice, then add the remaining ingredients, except the lemon twist, and shake until chilled.

Strain into a chilled cocktail glass and garnish with the lemon twist.

COCKTAIL NO. 31

のアビエーション

Takumi's
Aviation

PERFECT MOMO

This cocktail is a riff on the Perfect Lady, a gin-based classic that quietly packs some punch. In place of the peach liqueur that is normally mixed with the gin, momoshu is a simple way to introduce new notes while staying true to the original's flavours.

60 ML (¼ CUP) JAPANESE GIN
2 TABLESPOONS MOMOSHU
2 TABLESPOONS LEMON JUICE
1 EGG WHITE OR 2 TABLESPOONS AQUAFABA
ICE CUBES
WEDGE OF PEACH, TO GARNISH

Pour all the ingredients, except the ice and peach wedge, into a cocktail shaker and shake vigorously to emulsify the egg. Add ice and shake again until chilled.

Strain into a chilled cocktail glass and garnish with the peach wedge.

COCKTAIL NO. 32

完璧な桃

Perfect
Momo

TEA HOPPER

This cocktail doubles as a dessert. A take on the classic Grasshopper, this recipe has a lush and creamy texture, which is elevated by the addition of matcha. While the classic drink may have fallen in popularity, this twist is a delicious way to end a dinner party.

ICE CUBES
2 TABLESPOONS CREME DE CACAO
2 TABLESPOONS CREME DE MENTHE
2 TABLESPOONS DOUBLE (HEAVY) CREAM OR
    COCONUT CREAM
1 TEASPOON MATCHA POWDER
2 DASHES OF CHOCOLATE BITTERS (OPTIONAL)
MINT LEAVES, TO GARNISH

Fill a cocktail shaker with ice, then pour in the remaining ingredients, except the mint leaves, and shake vigorously until chilled.

Strain into a chilled cocktail glass and garnish with mint leaves.

ティーホッパー

Tea
Hopper

KURI ALEXANDER

The Brandy Alexander was very much in vogue in the 1970s, but the drink has since faded from popularity. Reinvention is always rife in the cocktail world, though, so what better way to bring the Alexander back than by simply replacing the creme de cacao with one of Japan's favourite autumnal flavours, chestnuts?

ICE CUBES
3 TABLESPOONS COGNAC
2 TABLESPOONS CHESTNUT LIQUEUR
2 TABLESPOONS CREAM
2 TEASPOONS SIMPLE SYRUP (PAGE 118)
GRATED NUTMEG, TO GARNISH

Fill a cocktail shaker with ice, then pour in the liquids and shake vigorously until chilled.

Strain into a chilled cocktail glass and garnish with nutmeg.

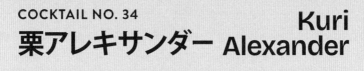

COCKTAIL NO. 34

栗アレキサンダー

Kuri Alexander

HOJICHA TODDY

Because hojicha is roasted, it has a distinct flavour. Rich, nutty and smooth, the tea perfectly complements whisky. When the nights grow cold, try the combination to keep cosy.

3 TABLESPOONS HOJICHA TEA LEAVES
200 ML (7 OZ) BOILING WATER
2 TABLESPOONS JAPANESE WHISKY
1 TABLESPOON HONEY
2 LEMON SLICES
1 CINNAMON STICK

In a teapot, steep the tea leaves in the water for 1 minute.

Strain the tea into a teacup, add in the whisky and honey and stir to combine.

Garnish with the lemon slices and cinnamon stick.

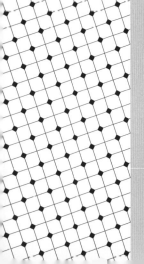

焙じ茶トディ

Hojicha Toddy

パート3 夜更かし

PART THREE

Late Nights

For nights that stretch over the hours and between bars, these drinks are great companions that will see you through from the first order to the last call.

HAIBORU

A favourite drink across izakaya, the refreshing Haiboru (highball) is made with only whisky, sparkling water and ice. But as with other Japanese traditions, there are many details to consider. A highly carbonated sparkling water and the choice of whisky are paramount, as is making sure the drink is served ice cold.

ICE CUBES
60 ML (¼ CUP) JAPANESE WHISKY
SPARKLING WATER, TO TOP
1 LEMON SLICE, TO GARNISH

Fill a highball glass with ice, then pour in the whisky.

To top up the drink, slowly pour sparkling water down the inside of the glass, to minimise foam. Stir gently to combine.

Garnish with the lemon slice.

COCKTAIL NO. 36

ハイボール　　　Haiboru

GULF STREAM

A very blue, very delicious Japanese cocktail, with a colour reminiscent of warm seas thanks to the inclusion of blue curacao. With its sweet, tropical taste, this drink is a fruity blend that'll sweep you away to sandy beaches, or the dancefloor.

ICE CUBES
2 TABLESPOONS VODKA
20 ML (¾ OZ) PEACH LIQUEUR
2 TEASPOONS BLUE CURACAO
50 ML (1¾ OZ) PINK GRAPEFRUIT JUICE
2 TEASPOONS PINEAPPLE JUICE

Fill a cocktail shaker with ice, then pour in the liquids and shake vigorously until chilled.

Strain into an ice-filled tumbler.

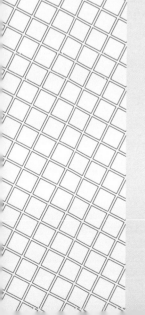

COCKTAIL NO. 37

ガルフ ストリーム

Gulf Stream

MISO-RITA

To transform the Margarita, miso is an excellent choice. Its richness introduces a warm depth to the salty, tangy classic. For an additional kick, try using shichimi togarashi to rim the glass.

SALT, TO RIM THE GLASS
2 LIME WHEELS, PLUS 2 TABLESPOONS LIME JUICE
ICE CUBES
3 TABLESPOONS TEQUILA
2 TABLESPOONS ORANGE LIQUEUR
1 TABLESPOON MISO SYRUP (PAGE 118)

Tip the salt into a shallow dish. Moisten the rim of a tumbler with one lime wheel, then dip or roll the edge of the glass in the salt to coat.

Fill a cocktail shaker with ice, then pour in the liquids and shake until chilled.

Strain into the prepared tumbler and garnish with the lime wheel.

味噌リータ   **Miso-rita**

CHU-HAI

While the Chu-hai originated in bars, it is now sold tinned in vending machines and stores around Japan. It is made with shochu – hence its name, a portmanteau of 'shochu' and 'highball'. This recipe is lemon-flavoured, but you can adjust with other fruit juices and syrups, or other flavours like Calpico. You can also adjust the amount of juice used, to suit your taste.

60 ML (¼ CUP) SHOCHU
2 TABLESPOONS LEMON JUICE, PLUS 1–2 LEMON WEDGES TO GARNISH
SIMPLE SYRUP, TO TASTE (OPTIONAL; PAGE 118)
ICE CUBES
180 ML (6 OZ) SPARKLING WATER

Pour the shochu, lemon juice and simple syrup, if using, into a highball glass and stir to combine.

Add ice to the glass. To top up the drink, slowly pour sparkling water down the inside of the glass, to minimise foam. Stir gently to combine.

Garnish with the lemon wedges.

チューハイ

Chu-hai

MELON SODA

Melon soda, with its unmistakable bright green shade, is a favourite soft drink in Japan. Its perfect blend of melon and fizz is delicious on a summer's day – particularly with a scoop of ice cream to finish the glass. This alcoholic version, which gets its melon flavour from Midori and its kick from shochu, is a grown-up twist on the classic.

ICE CUBES
2 TABLESPOONS SHOCHU
60 ML (¼ CUP) MIDORI
90 ML (3 OZ) LEMONADE (LEMON-LIME SODA)
MARASCHINO CHERRY, TO GARNISH

Fill a highball glass with ice cubes, then pour in the liquids and stir gently to combine.

Garnish with the cherry.

COCKTAIL NO. 40
メロンソーダ

Melon
Soda

MATCHA-HAI

Like the classic Haiboru (page 88), this Matcha-hai is prepared with whisky. The alcohol's woody depth suits the earthy, nutty complement of the tea: a refreshing way to finish any meal.

¼ TEASPOON MATCHA POWDER
3 TABLESPOONS JAPANESE WHISKY
1 TABLESPOON LEMON JUICE, PLUS LEMON TWIST
   TO GARNISH
ICE CUBES
SPARKLING WATER, TO TOP

Add the matcha, whisky and lemon juice to a highball glass and stir to combine.

Add ice to the glass. To top up the drink, slowly pour sparkling water down the inside of the glass, to minimise foam. Stir gently to combine.

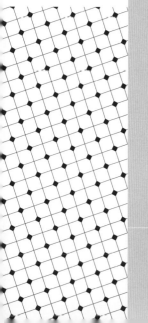

抹茶ハイ　　Matcha-hai

UMEBOSHI SOUR

In izakaya, you'll find variations of high balls that are prepared with umeboshi (pickled plums), which you can buy at Asian grocers. Some recipes are more sour, some more sweet. This one is flavoured with umeshu, which adds a very quaffable sweetness to the recipe.

PICKLED PLUM, TO GARNISH
ICE CUBES
2 TABLESPOONS SHOCHU
2 TABLESPOONS UMESHU
SPARKLING WATER, TO TOP

Add the pickled plum to a highball glass and muddle.

Add the ice, shochu and umeshu. To top up the drink, slowly pour sparkling water down the inside of the glass, to minimise foam. Stir gently to combine.

COCKTAIL NO. 42

梅干サワー

Umeboshi
Sour

SAKURA MARTINI

The soft pink hue of this Martini belies its inspiration: cherry blossoms. Japan's iconic flower infuses this drink through both the syrup and the gin: a delicious way to enjoy one of the country's most famous botanicals.

ICE CUBES
60 ML (¼ CUP) SAKURA GIN
3 TABLESPOONS SAKE
1 TEASPOON DRY VERMOUTH
1½ TEASPOONS SAKURA SYRUP
SAKURA BLOSSOM, TO GARNISH

Fill a mixing glass with ice, then pour in the liquids and stir until chilled.

Strain the drink into a chilled martini glass and garnish with the sakura blossom.

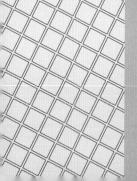

COCKTAIL NO. 43

桜マティーニ

Sakura
Martini

W A S A B I - R I T A

Wasabi has a distinctly sharp heat all its own, which is a delicious addition to Margaritas. On long nights, this is just the drink to wake up your senses.

WASABI SALT, TO RIM THE GLASS
2 LIME WEDGES, PLUS 2 TABLESPOONS LIME JUICE
ICE CUBES
3 TABLESPOONS TEQUILA
2 TABLESPOONS ORANGE LIQUEUR
1 TABLESPOON WASABI SYRUP (PAGE 119)

Tip the wasabi salt into a shallow dish. Moisten the rim of a tumbler with one lime wedge, then dip or roll the edge of the glass in the wasabi salt to coat.

Fill a cocktail shaker with ice, then pour in the liquids and shake until chilled.

Fill the prepared tumbler with ice, then strain in the drink from the shaker. Garnish with the second lime wedge.

COCKTAIL NO. 44

山葵リータ　Wasabi-rita

CASSIS ORANGE

This drink, which popularly appears on menus in Japan, is the perfect option for those who'd like to avoid feeling a little worse for wear in the morning. The delicious mix of the blackcurrant liqueur and orange juice has a low alcohol content, which also makes it a worthwhile addition to brunch menus

ICE CUBES
60 ML (¼ CUP) CREME DE CASSIS
150 ML (5 OZ) ORANGE JUICE
ORANGE TWIST, TO GARNISH

Fill a highball glass with ice cubes, then pour in the creme de cassis.

Finish with the orange juice and garnish with the orange twist.

カシス オレンジ

Cassis Orange

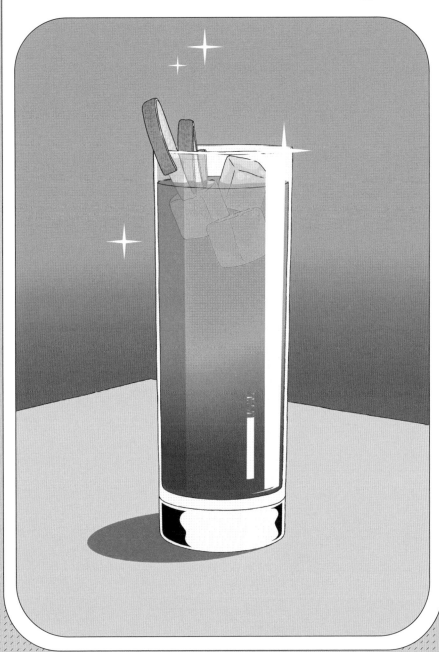

SAKETINI

A Vodka Martini is a great opportunity to use sake. The breadth of sakes available is vast, so if your cocktail cabinet houses more than one, it's worth comparing and contrasting the nuances of their flavours in at least two Saketinis.

ICE CUBES
70 ML (2¼ OZ) SAKE
1 TABLESPOON VODKA
½ TEASPOON DRY VERMOUTH
SLICE OF CUCUMBER, TO GARNISH

Fill a mixing glass with ice, then pour in the liquids and stir until chilled.

Strain the drink into a chilled martini glass.

Garnish with the cucumber slice.

酒ティーニ

Saketini

RYOKUCHA-HAI

Shochu mellowed with earthy green tea is easy to find in an izakaya: a simple drink for evenings when the summer humidity is high. While a barley shochu is recommended, different shochus are worth exploring, so experiment with different kinds to find your favourite.

ICE CUBES
2 TABLESPOONS SHOCHU
120 ML (4 OZ) GREEN TEA, CHILLED

Fill a highball glass with ice, then pour in the shochu and green tea and stir to combine.

緑茶ハイ　Ryokucha-hai

MIDORI GIN FIZZ

The Gin Fizz is transformed here by Midori and Calpico into the perfect drink for those after a pop of colour to brighten up the night. This frothy glass is a great option for those who prefer to dilute the melon liqueur's sweetness, while still maintaining its signature flavour.

1 TABLESPOON MIDORI
2 TABLESPOONS GIN
2 TABLESPOONS CALPICO, MELON FLAVOUR
1 TABLESPOON LEMON JUICE
20 ML (¾ OZ) SIMPLE SYRUP (PAGE 118)
1 EGG WHITE OR 2 TABLESPOONS AQUAFABA
ICE CUBES
SPARKLING WATER, TO TOP
3 MELON BALLS, TO GARNISH

Pour all the liquids, except the sparkling water, into a cocktail shaker, and shake vigorously to emulsify the egg. Add ice and shake until chilled.

Strain into a highball glass and top up with sparkling water.

Garnish with the melon balls.

COCKTAIL NO. 48

緑ジンフィズ

Midori
Gin Fizz

OOLONG-HAI

Yet another simple, refreshing drink common to izakaya. Your chosen ingredients will dictate the result – if you're unsure where to start, a sweet potato shochu is a great option for this simple, classic combination.

ICE CUBES
80 ML (2½ OZ) SHOCHU
120 ML (4 OZ) OOLONG TEA, CHILLED

Fill a highball glass with ice, then pour in the shochu and ooloong tea and stir to combine.

烏龍ハイ Oolong-hai

UP LATE

The Espresso Martini's kick from its caffeine and vodka never fails to get the conversation firing and the dancefloor packed. This version combines miso and whisky: a great accompaniment to any karaoke session.

ICE CUBES
40 ML (1¼ OZ) JAPANESE WHISKY
20 ML (¾ OZ) ESPRESSO, CHILLED
20 ML (¾ OZ) COFFEE LIQUEUR
1 TABLESPOON MISO SYRUP (PAGE 118)
3 COFFEE BEANS, TO GARNISH

Fill a cocktail shaker with ice, then pour in the liquids and shake vigorously until chilled.

Strain into a chilled martini glass and garnish with the coffee beans.

COCKTAIL NO. 50

夜更かし

Up
Late

Basics

While some of the syrups included here are sold in stores, they're all simple to make if you have the ingredients and time.

SIMPLE SYRUP
Makes 125 ml (½ cup)

110 G (4 OZ) CASTER (SUPERFINE) SUGAR

Combine the sugar and 125 ml (½ cup) of water in a small saucepan. Bring to the boil and stir until the sugar dissolves. Remove from the heat and allow to cool.

The simple syrup will keep in an airtight container in the fridge for up to 1 week.

GINGER SYRUP
Makes 125 ml (½ cup)

100 G (3½ OZ) GINGER, PEELED AND THINLY SLICED
110 G (4 OZ) CASTER (SUPERFINE) SUGAR

Combine the ginger, sugar and 125 ml (½ cup) of water in a saucepan. Bring to the boil and stir until the sugar dissolves. Remove from the heat and allow the ginger to steep until the syrup is cool.

Strain into a container, discarding the ginger.

The ginger syrup will keep in an airtight container in the fridge for up to 1 week.

MISO SYRUP
Makes 140 ml (4½ oz)

110 G (4 OZ) CASTER (SUPERFINE) SUGAR
12 G (½ OZ) WHITE MISO

Combine the sugar and 125 ml (½ cup) of water in a small saucepan. Bring to the boil and stir until the sugar dissolves. Remove from the heat, add the miso and stir until the miso dissolves.

The miso syrup will keep in an airtight container in the fridge for up to 1 week.

VANILLA SYRUP
Makes 125 ml (½ cup)

1 VANILLA BEAN, SPLIT LENGTHWAYS AND SEEDS SCRAPED
110 G (4 OZ) CASTER (SUPERFINE) SUGAR
¼ TEASPOON VANILLA EXTRACT

Combine the vanilla bean and seeds, sugar and 125 ml (½ cup) of water in a saucepan. Bring to the boil and stir until the sugar dissolves. Stir in the vanilla extract and set aside to cool.

Strain into a container, discarding the solids.

The vanilla syrup will keep in an airtight container in the fridge for up to 1 week.

WASABI SYRUP
Makes 130 ml (4½ oz)

125 ML (½ CUP) SIMPLE SYRUP
  (SEE OPPOSITE)
10 G (½ OZ) WASABI PASTE

In a bowl, combine the simple syrup and wasabi paste and use a stick blender to blend until the wasabi dissolves. Strain into a container, discarding any solids.

The wasabi syrup will keep in an airtight container in the fridge for up to 1 week.

WHIPPED CREAM
Makes 250 ml (1 cup)

250 ML (1 CUP) DOUBLE (HEAVY) CREAM
1½ TABLESPOONS ICING SUGAR
1 TEASPOON VANILLA EXTRACT

To make the whipped cream, whisk all the ingredients in a bowl until small peaks form.

The whipped cream will keep in an airtight container in the fridge for up to 3 days.

MATCHA CREAM
Makes 250 ml (1 cup)

250 ML (1 CUP) DOUBLE (HEAVY) CREAM
1½ TABLESPOONS ICING SUGAR
1 TABLESPOON MATCHA POWDER

To make the matcha cream, whisk all the ingredients in a bowl until small peaks form.

The matcha cream will keep in an airtight container in the fridge for up to 3 days.

FRUIT JELLIES
Makes approximately 80 squares

250 ML (1 CUP) FRUIT JUICE OF
  YOUR CHOICE
2 TEASPOONS AGAR AGAR POWDER
60 G (2 OZ) CASTER (SUPERFINE) SUGAR
250 ML (1 CUP) VODKA

In a saucepan, mix the juice, agar agar and sugar. Bring to the boil, stirring constantly. Continue to cook, stirring, for 2 minutes.

Remove from the heat and add the vodka, stirring to combine. Pour into a 25 x 15 cm (10 x 6 in) baking tin, and transfer to the fridge for 2 hours, or until set.

Once set, cut the fruit jelly into approximately 2 cm (¾ in) cubes.

The fruit jellies will keep in an airtight container in the fridge for up to 1 week.

MATCHA JELLIES
Makes approximately 80 squares

2 TEASPOONS AGAR AGAR POWDER
60 G (2 OZ) CASTER (SUPERFINE) SUGAR
2 TEASPOONS MATCHA POWDER
250 ML (1 CUP) JAPANESE WHISKY

In a saucepan, mix the agar agar, sugar and matcha powder with 250 ml (1 cup) of cold water. Bring to the boil, stirring constantly. Continue to cook, stirring, for 2 minutes.

Remove from the heat and add the whisky, stirring to combine. Pour into a 25 x 15 cm (10 x 6 in) baking tin, and transfer to the fridge for 2 hours, or until set.

Once set, cut the matcha jelly into approximately 2 cm (¾ in) cubes.

The matcha jellies will keep in an airtight container in the fridge for up to 1 week.

Index

Published in 2025 by Smith Street Books
Naarm (Melbourne) | Australia
smithstreetbooks.com

ISBN: 978-1-9230-4985-7

Smith Street Books respectfully acknowledges the Wurundjeri People of the Kulin Nation, who are the Traditional Owners of the land on which we work, and we pay our respects to their Elders past and present.

Publisher: Hannah Koelmeyer
Managing editor: Avery Hayes
Editor: Penny Mansley
Text: Gill Hutchison
Illustrations: Phil Constantinesco
Design concept: Mylène Mozas
Design for pages 4–5: George Saad
Design layout: Megan Ellis
Production manager: Aisling Coughlan

Printed & bound in China by C&C Offset Printing Co., Ltd.

Book 379
10 9 8 7 6 5 4 3 2 1